T0365468

IN EVERY

Season

An Interactive Devotional

K. L. JOHNSTON

This book is a work of non-fiction. Unless otherwise noted, the author and the publisher make no explicit guarantees as to the accuracy of the information contained in this book and in some cases, names of people and places have been altered to protect their privacy.

WestBow Press books may be ordered through booksellers or by contacting:

WestBow Press
A Division of Thomas Nelson & Zondervan
1663 Liberty Drive
Bloomington, IN 47403
www.westbowpress.com
844.714.3454

Because of the dynamic nature of the Internet, any web addresses or links contained in this book may have changed since publication and may no longer be valid. The views expressed in this work are solely those of the author and do not necessarily reflect the views of the publisher, and the publisher hereby disclaims any responsibility for them.

Any people depicted in stock imagery provided by Getty Images are models, and such images are being used for illustrative purposes only.
Certain stock imagery © Getty Images.

Interior Image Credit: K. L. Johnston

Scripture quotations are from the ESV® Bible (The Holy Bible, English Standard Version®), copyright © 2001 by Crossway, a publishing ministry of Good News Publishers. Used by permission. All rights reserved.

ISBN: 978-1-6642-0581-9 (sc)
ISBN: 978-1-6642-0582-6 (e)

Library of Congress Control Number: 2020917946

Print information available on the last page.

WestBow Press rev. date: 10/26/2020

WESTBOW
PRESS®
A DIVISION OF THOMAS NELSON
& ZONDERVAN

Dedication

Soli Deo Gloria

Acknowledgement

My thanks to my team at Westbow Press and to my friends and early readers, Ann Jackson and Susan Christie. Thanks to Lindy Liptak who has been an excellent big sister. Most of all thanks to my husband Joe who puts up with my absent mindedness, flight of ideas, and random sense of humor.

Using This Book

In Every Season is a sharing of meditations and interactions with God and the many surprising insights provided by the Holy Spirit. It is intended to be an interactive springboard for the reader's contemplative conversations with Him.

Parts One and Three are composed of poetry, photos, and scripture references. Each poem is grouped with an accompanying photo and scripture reference to present a complete meditation. This is where I share my experiences and moments of clarity brought about by the Holy Spirit. Your experience will be enriched if you pause to look up the scripture reference that captions the photo.

Parts Two and Four are open ended meditations on scripture. Here you can find my meditations on scripture and add your own thoughts and insights. You can contemplate the photos, look up the scripture reference, agree or disagree with my interpretations, and write in the spaces left open for the Reader's Meditations. Use this as a place for your own thoughts to take flight. Talk to God about it and discuss your ideas with Him. He allows us that privilege.

My hope is that you will use this book to make your conversations with God living and valid. There are experiences common to all of us, but God walks each of us through them in unique ways. I've brought you some of my prayers and vision of the Creation in these meditations and hope that you will add yours to the glory of God.

May God bless you through these pages.
K. L. Johnston

Contents

Praise

Part One

"The chief end of man is to glorify God and enjoy Him forever."
The Westminster Shorter Catechism

Psalm 66:1-2

Evangelium

My evangelium should be like the song of birds
only heard because it is intrinsic.

Because I can't help it,
it is so much a part of me.

Because it is gut wrenching,
pushing my heart and lungs
until it rises up on grace, not ego
and with the Spirit of new life

it should send me out each morning
in a day I have never known before,
leaving baggage behind,
following adventures,
sharing treasures.

Job 11:17-18

Morning Devotion

Thankful for this good night's sleep,
for waking with the light
as morning creeps over the walls.
Grateful for the silence that is not quiet
in the deeps of gold and blue as an echo
of angel song in the First Light.

I would keep and bind these voices to me
but I am broken and forgetful and cannot
hold glory in my head or hand for too long.

This is the gift, this singing silence.
This light that seeps in and pins me down
holds me steady.
For a few moments my world is balanced.
All is right.
And I am fed
song, color, light.

Genesis 2:5-9

Misting Rain

Almost, I do not go out into the garden.
The morning is warm, the misting rain is inconvenient, sure
to make the air muggy, the earth sticky, the tasks at hand
slightly more difficult.

But I have the itch to feel the earth
between my fingers and under my toes,
to stretch the creative muscles that wield a spade.
I armor up: boonie hat, gloves, garden clogs,

and Ahh!
The spade slides so easily. The plants settle
snug in their new homes. There is no glare,
no threat of sunburn.
I do not even break a sweat.

I ask was there a mist over that first garden?
and were all inconveniences such blessings?

1 Samuel 3:1-16

Unsleepy

The house is dark except for the night light in the hall.
The night is quiet except for the dog's soft snoring.
My Dear One is a comforting bulk beside me
having taken all the extra pillows.

I am safe and content.
I am not Samuel to hear Your voice calling me aloud.
But You might as well have,
now that You have wakened me to prayers.

Where do I begin?
I feel no urgency. I am singularly untroubled.
So I begin to begin by pondering You
in Your creation, in Your love, in Your plans made known so far.

Surrounded by these created loves You have given me
I come happily into Your greater love
to give You thanks.

Maybe that's all that this wakefulness is about:
recognizing You in the time of contentment
and giving thanks.

James 5:7

Salad Blessing

Bless the seed and bless the fruit,
bless the stem and bless the root,
bless the hungry mouths You feed,
bless us Lord as we have need.

Bless the flower, bless the blade,
bless the hands that wield the spade,
bless the meek and commonplace,
bless us Lord and grant us grace.

Matthew 10:29

Sparrow

There is a part of me
that is small and joyful,

surviving a life
in a broken-hearted world

by continuing to remain
joyful and small.

Job 12: 7-10

Fugue

The cacophony of voices is
easier to ignore since we have lost the gift of languages.
I must concentrate to listen to the separate lines of dialogue,
to separate the meanings.

I sometimes shout at the storm, the waves,
the birds, the chittering squirrels
and the distant yelping coyotes.
One at a time! Please.

And then I must laugh, or else
weep at my foolishness.
They are so urgent and so earnest,
all always saying the same thing….

Soli Deo Gloria.

Mark 1:13

Consolation

They came to joy over him:
purring, panting, rolling over for belly rubs;
the jackal and the raven, the lizards
lining up to stare with their unblinking eyes
and the lion of the desert
grooming with a rough tongue the Lion of Judah.

They came to joy over him:
the beings of light and power and eternal song
bringing him sustenance and news of the last 40 days
lauding
the laying down of this burden of temptation.
Bringing praise.

The fulcrum of all time and Creation
sat on the desert floor and made merry
among the beasts and the angels.
It was only the creation that hung in the balance,
the perfect balance.
Things were for that moment
revealed just the way they were planned.

Matthew 26: 48-54

Gethsemene Perspective

From this cold world gazing outward
blackest night is pierced only on occasion by glory,
starshine the briefest glimpse of grace vouchsafed to hearts
uncertain, aching, agape in awe.

Who else would have this broken- hearted world?
No one else comes near us in the darkness except to devour.
A vulture's wing of hunger stifles one small world waiting
flailing on the fulcrum of one starry night
and a weeping dawn.

The host was ready, tensed for the battle and the charge
then ordered to stand down;
awestruck by the alternative, the empty cup and broken bread,
the stumbling bloody uphill climb,
the ripping veil, the enemy wailing at nightfall gone awry.

Out there in the stranger wilder dawn the stars still shine
on other worlds unfallen, the guardian of each one bending so close
curious, ready, exulting;
to see if we will look into the empty tomb
while feathers of glory flame most wildly in this atmosphere.

Isaiah 42:9, Luke 22:19-20, Revelation 21:4-5

Planned

Six inches of soil and rain.
That's all it takes to achieve sustenance;
starting the process of providing for need,
growing the wheat and the grapes.

Growing things is my constant piece of work,
that and remembering;
remembering what is broken,
remembering what is poured out,
remembering to rejoice in partaking.

There are still dustbowls.
There are still droughts and floods.
But the one who created is also the One
who is continually creating anew;

not mending a tear, not patching a hole,
not fixing a leak
but all things new.

Meetings

Part Two

"The prayer of a Christian is not an attempt to force God's hand, but a humble acknowledgement of helpless dependence… what we do every time we pray is to confess our own impotence and God's sovereignty."
J. I. Packer: Evangelism and the Sovereignty of God

Genesis 1:1

In the beginning God created the heavens and the earth.

If this verse isn't true, then nothing else in all of the earth matters. If You are not the Fact behind the Creation then Your book is just another mythology.

What a terrible abyss this would be, Lord!

But You made Your Creation to reveal yourself in wonders and mysteries. Mountains rise toward heaven and light plays downward, destroying shadows.

I can see Your hand in every aspect of it: the gentle, the beautiful and the fierce. I love Your creation because it is a reflection of You.

Your story goes on forever, and everything You have made is a part of it: platypuses and atomic particles, the Marianas Trench and cumulus clouds, and me. I'm part of it too.

Nehemiah 9:6

You alone are the LORD. You made the heavens, even the highest heavens, and all their starry host, the earth and all that is on it, the seas and all that is in them. You give life to everything, and the multitudes of heaven worship You.

Keep me looking up!

When I look up I see the clouds and the thunderstorms, the brilliant sun and the filtered light coming through the leaves of the shade trees. I see the horizon over the sea as it changes minute by minute, day by day.

I see glimpses of You everywhere.

You have given me directions and signs if I will just look up to You for guidance. At the highest level, all of the inhabitants of Your heavens know this and it is their joy to worship You.

I want to join in. Please Lord, keep me looking up.

Psalm 84:3-4

Even the sparrow finds a home, and the swallow a nest for herself, where she may lay her Young, at Your altars, O Lord of hosts, my King and my God. Blessed are those who dwell in Your house, eversinging Your praise!

Some folks think of swallows as pests, nesting in inconvenient places, making a mess and swooping everywhere. But You created that swooping flight so that they can catch and eat mosquitoes on the wing and You welcomed the pests to Your altars.

Not everyone has a good opinion of me either, especially those I've disappointed, or who see no purpose in my flights of imagination.

Yet You welcome me to Your heart and to Your altar, even though I can be annoying. You allow me to make a home with You in sacred spaces; spaces where You have led me to live.

Even though my purpose may not be as beautiful as the flight of a swallow or the song of a sparrow, I know that Your plan encompasses all my deeds. I thank You for accepting my offerings and for allowing me to come home to You.

Hosea 6:3

Let us know; let us press on to know the Lord; his going out is sure as the dawn; he will come to us as the showers, as the spring rains that water the earth."

It doesn't take long for things to wither in this World. Heat and cold, time and entropy can be destroyers. Whether it's a house plant or a life calling, they will wither and die with lack of care.

When my heart is choked with dust and bitterness You care for me. In the stale and dry times of my life I turn to You, and through Your Word and by Your Spirit You send Your gifts to renew my hopes and bring me life.

Send the rains of Your love!

Praise Your name, Your love flows down to me!

I will splash in the puddles of Your amazing gifts. I will bathe in the streams of Your abundant love. I will dance in the light of Your dawn.

James 1:17

Every good and perfect gift is from above, coming down from the Father of the heavenly lights, who does not change like shifting shadows.

It is easy to accept pale and shadowy imitations of Your goodness when I cannot see Your face clearly. When shadows fall, it is easy to lose my way.

But there are no shadows in Your love. You only reveal more and more of Yourself in Your Creation, through Your Word, and by Your Holy Spirit.

You give me practical gifts that are sometimes hard to accept, that teach me perseverance and patience. And You give me surprising moments of delight and laughter. But Your gifts are not random.

Your gifts become part of who I am and what I do, shaping me in Your image. They become the foundations of thanksgiving, starting with thanks for the air I breathe and the earth I stand on, continuing into the eternal Hosanna.

John 4:13-14

Psalm 32:7

Psalm 147: 7-11

Proverbs 8:22-31

Isaiah 65:25

1 Corinthians 3:16

Do You not know that You are God's temple and that God's Spirit dwells in You?

Decorated in gold and silver and bronze laid over costly woods, smelling of sweet incense, inhabited by priests who strode between the images of the towering cherubim; that was Your first temple at Jerusalem. At Your direction it was crafted by human hands to be a place of beauty like the world had never seen before.

It was the majestic place of the Holy of Holies, of prayers and worship, and the place of sacrifice. This is what You want me to become? This is where You want to dwell?

Flesh and bones are only the beginnings of the eternal body You are creating in me. You are rebuilding me from the inside out.

As Your Holy Spirit lives in me You will give me joy in returning all my treasures to Your glory. Grant me the courage to live with Your Spirit in the place of sacrifice. In Your time and by Your grace let me meet You striding with assurance in prayer and worship among Your cherubim.

1 Thessalonians 4:11-12

… and to aspire to live quietly, and to mind Your own affairs, and to work with Your hands, as we instructed You, so that You may walk properly before outsiders and be dependent on no one.

Living quietly and minding my own business is difficult when those things don't come naturally. I can be both nosy and noisy, as You well know. Forgive me.

As I go about my work in this World, I am relieved that You are constantly with me, standing at my shoulder. Knowing that You are standing beside me is a reminder that You also stand by my co-workers. And that working to the best of my ability is an act of devotion.

Let my devotion to You show as I go out and make a living, depending totally on You for my daily bread, so that I am Your representative. Let it show in all my dealings with strangers and co-workers, so that if they think well of me, it is based on how they see Your Spirit in me.

But in this daily apprenticeship for eternity, Your good opinion is the one I seek.

Luke 5:15-16

But now even more the report about him went abroad, and great crowds gathered to hear him and to be healed of their infirmities. But he would withdraw to desolate places and pray.

If I follow your practices, I will find You in the desolate places and in the mountains. I will find you in the gardens and the farmlands.

These are the places where the only other voices I hear are coming from your Creation: birdsong and running water, wind in the trees and the occasional calling of the beasts of the field. These are the places of quiet where I can pray without distraction, focusing on you and hearing your voice. In the wilderness the imprint of Your path is clear and I can follow in Your footsteps.

And when I return to the World, speak loudly to me so that there is no confusion about whose voice I am following. Let there be no confusion between Your voice, the Creation and the World. When I return to the World, let me carry Your voice inside me, so filled with Your Word that my speech is purified and overflowing. Let me sing along with Your song of Creation in my heart.

Matthew 6:9-11

"This, then, is how You should pray: "'Our Father in heaven, hallowed be Your name, Your kingdom come, Your will be done, on earth as it is in heaven.

The scariest thing You ever said to me was "OK child, if You want it so much, have Your own way."

I'm sorry I had to learn the hard way that Your will is perfect and wise and mine is not and never will be.

I know enough now to understand that I can follow You with assurance, even through painful times, and scary times. Even through the times when I am blindsided and just want to know what in the world is going on. And I understand now that I cannot take credit for those times when, wonder of wonders, everything comes out right.

Your kingdom is here and You have made me a part of it. You have rescued me, but this is no fairy tale. You are full of power and majesty, love and grace, but this is no myth! This is the great adventure of Your living love in action, and I am overawed that You, who know my deepest failings, want me to be part of Your kingdom on this earth.

Philippians 4:8

Finally, brothers and sisters, whatever is true, whatever is noble, whatever is right, whatever is pure, whatever is lovely, whatever is admirable—if anything is excellent or praiseworthy—think about such things.

I learn to recognize your face first in the beauty of Your Creation, the things my five senses can grasp.

Stone and tree are basic things I take for granted, they are so stable and enduring. Once I understand how they reflect your heart, I begin to grasp the idea of You in wind and light. And it is the Light of the World and the Breath of Your Spirit that reveal so much more of who you are.

In the light of who You are I begin to see You in the good things in this broken world, in Your graciousness and laughter, in the quirks of humanity, in the striving to imitate Your creativity.

I begin to look into the faces of everyone I meet, searching them, not to condemn, but to find the flame of Your light in them. You are training my world view to correct my thinking vision to see clearly in the light of Your Word.. By Your grace, one day I will be able to bear standing in the full Light of your Glory.

Reader's Meditations

Realization

Part Three

'We may ignore, but we cannot evade the presence of God. The world is crowded with Him. He walks everywhere incognito."

C.S. Lewis

Isaiah 61:1-3

Left Behind

Since I left my parents' house I've
seldom stayed in any one house for long,
I have tried to leave each place
better. I've made the necessary repairs,
replacing roofs, reclaiming floors,
keeping things reasonably clean even with the kids,
dogs, cats, hamsters, goldfish.

I've done my best work in the gardens,
planting for the futures I will not see,
for people I will not know.
Evergreens will out-last
several lives of men
and have their own peculiar beauties.

I pass by the places I have left
behind and recognize these children of the earth,
like the midwife who passes
an adult on the street, remembering a squalling infant
swaddled for the first time.

Saying all this gives me too much importance.
I gave my sweat as a gift.
Seeing the gift grown and still giving
gives me joy.

Romans 8:19-25

Yellowstone

I walked blithe and unthinking into a land
where the hand of God is obvious and active;
comforting myself not in spirit but in technologies, a down parka
offering fragile insulation in the swirling matrix of snow, melting
mid-air over fumaroles and geysers.
Steaming cracks in the skin of the planet
boil, a rainbow colored soup of thriving,
microscopic thermophiles in the liquid stone bubbling to the surface.

I am uneasily reminded that creation is a time of travail.
Head bowed, I leave retreating footprints in snow
just a cosmic moment away from new earth.

Colossians 3:13-14

Stealing the Rose

If you steal a rose
(not that I would do such a thing) the thorns
slip under your skin.
It's a festering reminder
that maybe you should bake a batch of cookies
to take across the fence
and confess to being overcome by beauty.

Then you can begin tweezing out the prickles,
watch without envy the roses
blooming in y our neighbor's garden
and breathe in forgiveness like a perfumed gift.

I Corinthians 12:4-6

Frenemy

It is as silly

for me to enumerate

anything I might love about You

as it is foolish for me to name

what annoys me most in You.

Let it be enough
that God made us
and I am learning to rejoice in his creation.

Jeremiah 29:11

The X-Ray

This is a photo of pain
no less painful for being accidental.
This is not a hangnail or the stub of a toe.
This may be a tragedy.

This is a picture of agony blossoming over a brain,
into the points of awareness.

But it is only the picture of a moment:
the picture of the moment when we start over
when we can begin to make plans,
when we can know what we are hoping for,
when we can know how we will be blessed
in spite of the moment.

Micah 6:8

No Goodbye

I never saw my father's face in death.
They closed the casket before I could make it home
and after the first fifteen years of shock, I was glad.

My sister said it looked like some old geezer
had stolen his clothes and was sleeping in them.

Now through slow discovery
when I wish I could ask his advice, I still see him clearly.
He's just stepped out:
he's hilling up the potatoes, or chopping wood or
he's sitting at his desk, book in hand, mulling over the Reformation.
Knowing him, he could be up to some mischief to make my mother laugh
or working a deal,
bringing Michael's troops the best malted batch of the angel's share.

I know he is busy. Generally I know
what advice he would give me from his standing among the blessed.
The remembrance of these things would be obscured
without the gift of the closed coffin.

I Peter 2:9

London 1976

Coming up from the underground station
at Kensington are three bare flights,
blank and bland and concrete.

There is no sunlight penetrating,
no street noise, but today the music of a flute.

Glad daylight touches the second level, and with that tune
almost knocks me backwards.
There is a flower seller there
with baskets of gold and royal blue fanning the light.

The musician stands at street level,
eyes closed as he plays.
The flute case open at his feet
catches an occasional offering.

My pence jingled there too.
I wish it had been more.
More in keeping with what he gave me
and the ever present question: What child is this?
I have kept with me all this time.

Psalm 51:10-12

Rebellion

O God my Father, and my Lord
I fail to come to You, say I'm bored and miserable
in daily life. I blame You for a world of strife
when I'm the only one to blame.
I squirm away from You in shame, reject Your joy,
turn from Your face, unworthy of redeeming grace,

daring to challenge You in Your might; disobedient,
arrogant, fallen, quite the rebel,
ignoring the happier gentle child that co-exists with pride grown wild
inside my skin. I'm drained and tired from the struggle
of fighting these desires.

Guide me to letting my Self go, gift me Your stillness,
Your spirit's slow and steady goodness.
Warm my soul, grant me Your peace and make me whole.

Lord in this day and in this place
I beg forgiveness, peace, and grace.

Job 22: 27-28

Decision in Paradise

It's forever one hour from tomorrow here.

The lion dancers claim the streets again,
the eighth holiday this year …. all the evils
still not placated by incense,
not frightened by fireworks.

It's all laid out for me, twenty- two stories down.
The beauty of the view secondary to the sweat on my neck.

Eighty-one degrees at sunset and I cannot open my window.
I have watched this night come forward. There was no twilight.
If there was a green flash on the horizon I missed it.
Trade winds won't cool the towers and man- made air has failed.

At the greatest distance, runway lights arrow away from the city
and every rising light I wish were mine,
blessed on its way across this terrible horizon of blank water.

Lion dancers din their way to the next block.
My scalp shivers a little, looking out from this height.
I'm wondering where to put my faith to see tomorrow.

Psalm 30: 11-12

Evening Prayers for Fukushima

The theme of the flower show was "fly me to the moon"
My unwilling entry fell short: a pleasure becoming a burden and a trial,
the moribana fragile next to florist blooms and massive urns.
Seeing my ephemeral offering through a judge's eye
gave me a fleeting jolt. Had no one watched the News?

First there was the sassafras, blooming on bare branches,
slanting backward over the bowl of still water,
(if Your bowl is sixteen inches Your branch should be twenty-four.
I got that right)
the bursting blooms like sky rockets.
Apparently the judge was not impressed,
or had never looked closely at sassafras, limb or blossom.
Her critique said the line lacked strength.

Then there were the iris; purple and common and antique,
treasured weeds, hence a proliferation.
These impressed her.
One of them was crushed in travel so I turned the blossom inside out.
This was judged to have meaning.

(Evening Prayers for Fukushima cont.)

Lastly there were stones;
black river rock to hold the flowers in place, blue black
granite for balance.
These also appealed. She did not discredit them.

I meant to say that prayers should rise up
past the moon
for the homeless and bereft and mourning.
That joy should be set free in prayer
from the compassionate for the living
for strength to grow and bloom again.

The vision of stone and water,
of sky touched with sassafras fire
did not translate well, a failed communication,
the failure judged entirely mine.
Still, second place. Against all judgements
prayer will rise.

Reader's Meditations

Presence

Part Four

There is a freedom that comes from being who we are in God and resting in God that enables us to bring something truer to the world than all of our doing. Sabbath keeping helps us to live within our limits, because on the sabbath, in many different ways, we allow ourselves to be the creatures in the presence of our Creator.

Dr. Ruth Haley Barton, Sacred Rhythms

Acts 17: 23-25

The God who made the world and everything in it, being Lord of heaven and earth, does not live in temples made by man, nor is he served by human hands, as though he needed anything, since he himself gives to all mankind life and breath and everything.

It is so evident by the works of Your hands that You have no need of me, or of anything that I can make or do. From the depths of the ocean to the outrageous beauties of the rising and setting sun, Your works proclaim Your majesty, Your might, and Your creativity.

I cannot create something with my hands that will outlast even the generations of humanity.

Yet You created me to have joy. You don't live in buildings of stone or brick, because Your Holy Spirit lives in me. It is Your Spirit that gives me life and love and purpose.

You don't need me, Father, but oh how I need You! I have that in common with everyone I meet.

This understanding is the beginning of knowing You and the complexity and completeness of Your love. This understanding is the beginning of loving my neighbor as much as I love myself.

Ecclesiastes 3:1

For everything there is a season, and a time for every matter under heaven:

You made this thing we call time when you put the sun and the moon in motion. You worked Your will, a delicate artistry, accompanied by the chorus of heavenly voices.

You gave me the gift of seasons on this turning earth and the gift of language to name my years, days, and hours. You gave me seasons of the heart also.

So often Your word calls for me to be patient, to wait on You. Time seems to be such a fixed thing in my life that it obscures Your plan. It can be a tyrant, meeting deadlines, watching calendars and timetables and being on time for this and for that.

You are greater than time. You stand outside the seasons and all things work to fulfill Your creative vision and Your creative and loving plan for me. When I wait on You, I have the peace of knowing that all of my moments are Yours to control. I praise You for all my times and for all my seasons.

Isaiah 40:31

But they who wait for the LORD shall renew their strength; they shall mount up with wings like eagles; they shall run and not be weary; they shall walk and not faint.

My naturalist friend calls it kettling, this swooping and circling flight of raptors. I wonder what purpose this lazy ballet serves, what it feels like to ride those air currents? I know they are watchful, studying the landscape, keeping their eyes on food, water, and survival.

It looks as if they are enjoying going about the daily business of being an eagle - just as You created them to be. If I had wings, I would unfurl them and soar too, proclaiming Your majesty.

This daily business of waiting on Your will is an activity, not a void. You strengthen my flight muscles by filling my waiting with scripture and prayer and listening to your Spirit and walking with You. Waiting here in this Creation is part of my apprenticeship for heaven. Teach me more. Let me practice my joy now, enjoying You.

Ecclesiastes 3:11

He has made everything beautiful in its time. Also, he has put eternity into man's heart, yet so that he cannot find out what God has done from the beginning to the end.

How miraculous it is to find that I am neither unlovely nor unloved in Your eyes.

You have crafted those things that are eternal and true and Your breath of life runs through it all. The wonderful, the strange, the brilliant and the fierce all reflect some aspect of Your nature.

There is no beginning and no end to Your love and deep inside I know this, but daily life presses in on me. I sometimes want to ask You "when is my time?"

I long to understand You. I catch glimpses of the beauty You create in everything and everyone. There are things You have done that pierce my heart and leave me in wonder. I can even grasp the rudiments of Your plans for me, for all of Your sons and daughters. My understanding is imperfect, yet I rejoice in Your voice when You say to me "Your time is now!"

Ecclesiastes 8:15

So I commend the enjoyment of life, because there is nothing better for a person under the sun than to eat and drink and be glad. Then joy will accompany them in their toil all the days of the life God has given them under the sun.

You rested on the seventh day and You have commanded me to do the same. You have given me days of rest enabling me to enjoy You and the wonders You created. Within all the days You have given me are moments of Sabbath if I will only look for them and rest in You.

You created holidays and Holy Days with us humans in mind. Celebrations and thanksgivings were Your idea and creation. What fun!

All this enjoyment comes from You and is given freely. Part of my calling is to give joy back to You in praise and worship so that any day can become a Sabbath. Any day I can walk in Your light. Any day I can praise Your name.

Ecclesiastes 11:1

Proverbs 3:3

Luke 8: 23-25

Matthew 6: 25-34?

Luke 11:36

Lamentations 3:20-22

My soul continually remembers it and is bowed down within me. But this I call to mind, and therefore I have hope: The steadfast love of the Lord never ceases; his mercies never come to an end.

You have brought me through hard times and walked with me from darkness into light. Now I can enjoy the gifts You have given me, and bless Your name.

Sometimes my own memories rise up and try to drag me under, a riptide sweeping the sand from under my feet. I feel guilty, or anxious, or overwhelmed by memories of things that happened long ago.

You are my rescuer! My memory holds other things besides the darkness, gifts from You that bring me joy. And I remember that You are the one who commanded obedience from the sea and the storm and said "Peace. Be still."

Beneath the shifting sands and the pulling tide I feel the immovable rock of Your love holding me up. You are there steadying me, and I can stand firm. And I reach for Your hand in the joyous anticipation that is hope.

Matthew 11:28-29

Come to me, all who labor and are heavy laden, and I will give you rest. Take my yoke upon you, and learn from me, for I am gentle and lowly in heart, and you will find rest for your souls.

When I sit still and rest with You I can feel the beating of Your heart. Everywhere in Creation there is a rhythm: birth and death, tides, seasons, sunrise to sunset. I settle into the great, slow, deep peace that You give.

I am brought to the realization of how you fill all things, that beyond this life and this planet Your breath of life still pulses between the stars; it's what gave them the breath to sing for joy at the Creation.

You have given me the privilege of just sitting still with my Creator, my Rescuer, and my Guardian. It is beautiful, but I can bear it for only a little while. This fidgety flesh of mine begins to make demands to go and busy myself with ephemeral things.

Your breath of life is so great and slow and deep that I take some of Your peace with me as I go about my day. Hopefully that peace will spill over, splash out, flow into the world through me. And I will return to You again to be renewed, a part of the rhythm of Your eternal breath.

Zephaniah 3:17

The Lord Your God is in your midst, a mighty one who will save; he will rejoice over you with gladness; he will quiet You by his love; he will exult over you with loud singing.

Your Spirit walks among us. What a shivery realization that is, that You are right here with me.

It is incredible to me that You rejoice over me. I am so small, so broken, so defensive that I cannot even hear You without the voice of Your Spirit in my ear.

And now I know something new from Your Word, because I never knew before that You sing.

Your created ones, the angels and King David and Simeon the priest sang for You. Daniel and Miriam and Mary sang for you.

It was Your song first. You sing over me, the good Father, rocking me, quieting me, singing to me of Your love. Open my ears to hear this Lord!

Ezekiel 36:26

I will give you a new heart and put a new spirit in You; I will remove from you your heart of stone and give you a heart of flesh.

Three times You asked Peter if he loved You, once for each time the cock crowed. I know You have faced betrayal.

You wept over the death of Lazarus, so I know You have suffered loss.

You prayed to Your Father to take that cup from You. I know You have faced fear.

And yet You still loved me enough to die and return for me, loved us all enough to rescue us.

I thought I had to keep my heart safe to survive and be whole. Betrayal, loss, and fear make for a hard and stony heart, my Lord. And yet when Your Spirit moves He makes me cry to You for a warm and beating heart again; a rescued heart, a heart of flesh and love. Break my heart Lord! Break my heart.

Isaiah 60:1-3

Arise, shine, for Your light has come, and the glory of the Lord has risen upon You. For behold, darkness shall cover the earth, and thick darkness the peoples; but the Lord will arise upon You, and his glory will be seen upon You. And nations shall come to Your light, and kings to the brightness of Your rising.

Oh! You have called me!

The shadow of darkness that presses down on all Your Creation presses down on me too. But You made plans long ago for the coming of the Light and You allow me to walk with You in the Light.

I hear Your voice in Your Word. I see Your plan in the Creation. I feel Your love through Your Spirit.

This is not just my story. I am nobody by the World's standards, but You have plans for nations and rulers and have made me part of them.

Am I ready for the adventure, Lord? I don't feel ready. But miraculously You have raised me up and here I am by Your love and grace.

Reader's Meditations

Jude 24 - 25

About the Author

K. L. Johnston received a BA in English with a History minor from the University of South Carolina, Aiken. She worked in a wide variety of occupations and callings from make-up artist to gallery owner and family historian. She is now retired from her final venture of dealing in art and antiques.

Ms. Johnston is an ordained deacon in her home church where she helped develop their prayer program and serves as a teacher and classroom facilitator. Her poetry, devotional prayers and photography have appeared in small literary magazines, church newsletters and in-house magazines.

A mom and a grandmother, she lives with her husband in the sandhills of South Carolina near the Savannah River. She enjoys exploring the world with her camera, writing, and gardening under the careful supervision of her two dogs and three cats.

Printed in the United States
By Bookmasters